# Catholic Update
## *guide to*
# The Mass

D1211230

MARY CAROL KENDZIA,
Series Editor

**ST. ANTHONY MESSENGER PRESS**
Cincinnati, Ohio

Cover and book design by Mark Sullivan
Cover image © Getty Images | Jupiterimages

LIBRARY OF CONGRESS CATALOGING-IN-PUBLICATION DATA

Catholic update guide to the mass / Mary Carol Kendzia, series
editor.

p. cm. — (Catholic update guides)

Includes bibliographical references.

ISBN 978-1-61636-004-7 (alk. paper)

1. Lord's Supper—Catholic Church. 2. Mass. I. Kendzia,
Mary Carol.

BX2230.3.C38 2011

234'.163—dc22

2011003952

Published by St. Anthony Messenger Press

28 W. Liberty St.

Cincinnati, OH 45202

www.AmericanCatholic.org

www.SAMPBooks.org

Printed in the United States of America.
Printed on acid-free paper.
11 12 13 14 15   5 4 3 2 1

# Contents

# *About This Series*

The Catholic Update guides take the best material from our best-selling newsletters and videos to bring you up-to-the-minute resources for your faith. Topically arranged for these books, the words you'll find in these pages are the same clear, concise, authoritative information you've come to expect from the nation's most trusted faith formation series. Plus, we've designed this series with a practical focus—giving the "what," "why," and "how to" for the people in the pews.

The series takes the topics most relevant to parish life— e.g., the Mass, sacraments, Scripture, the liturgical year—and draws them out in a fresh and straightforward way. The books can be read by individuals or used in a study group. They are an invaluable resource for sacramental preparation, RCIA participants, faith formation, and liturgical ministry training, and are a great tool for everyday Catholics who want to brush up on the basics.

The content for the series comes from noted authors such as Thomas Richstatter, O.F.M., Lawrence Mick, Leonard Foley, O.F.M., Carol Luebering, William H. Shannon, and others. Their theology and approach is grounded in Catholic practice and tradition, while mindful of current Church practice and teaching. We blend each author's style and approach into a voice that is clear, unified, and eminently readable.

Enrich your knowledge and practice of the Catholic faith with the helpful topics in the Catholic Update Guide series.

*Mary Carol Kendzia*
*Series Editor*

# *Introduction*

At the Last Supper, Jesus told his disciples, "Do this in memory of me." For centuries the Church has been faithful to this command through the celebration of the Mass.

The Mass is the central mystery of our Catholic, Christian faith. But what *is* the Mass? What does it mean? Does it really make a difference in our everyday lives? Why should we go? And, with all the changes in the Mass, *how* should we go?

This book will help you investigate these questions and others. By discussing a little of the history of the Mass and the rich blessings it offers, we hope you'll find your own understanding of what the Mass is and why you should go. And, by walking you through the parts of the Mass, including the changes in the new translation of the Roman Missal, we hope to offer you a little more confidence in knowing how to go and what to say when you get there.

You'll find that many times in these pages we talk about the Mass as a meal. This isn't meant to diminish the meaning of the Mass or make it seem more commonplace, but it is meant to let you know that you have a place at the table. We hope that you'll experience the Church in a new way—not as some unapproachable heavenly institution, nor as a flawed human institution, but as a home. Your home.

Whether your faith is newly minted, slightly out of practice, or decades old, your faith—our faith—is the only ticket you need to the family banquet. Join us for Mass: There's always room at this table.

# CHAPTER ONE

# What Is the Mass?

The Mass has been described as the "source and summit" of our Catholic faith, but just what is it we're celebrating every Sunday? In this chapter, Tom Richstatter, O.F.M., shares how his understanding of the Mass has evolved and how he understands and teaches about it today.

\*\*\*

Fifty years ago, when I received Holy Communion for the first time, I think I could have explained the Eucharist in five minutes. As a child, I could answer all the catechism questions. I got straight As in religion class.

Twenty years later, when I said Mass for the first time, I *knew* what Eucharist was all about. After all, I was a priest. Priests know those things. But trying to explain the Eucharist in just a few pages now seems to me to be an impossible task. What I can do is to give you a key which may unlock for you a richer understanding of the Eucharist.

That key is simply to deepen our understanding of the Mass by balancing its elements of Good Friday, Holy Thursday, and Easter Sunday.

## *Balancing Good Friday, Holy Thursday and Easter Sunday*

Balancing the images of Good Friday, Holy Thursday and Easter Sunday (sacrifice, banquet, and unity of creation) is not an easy task. Sometimes I feel like a juggler at the circus trying to keep three objects in the air at once. I am no good at juggling three objects. Yet, I think the Church is asking us to keep all three of these ideas balanced in our minds-just as the opening paragraph of the Second Vatican Council's treatment of Eucharist very carefully balances the three:

At the Last Supper [Holy Thursday], on the night when he was betrayed, our Savior instituted the eucharistic sacrifice of his Body and Blood. He did this in order to perpetuate the sacrifice of the cross [Good Friday] through– out the centuries until he should come again and in this way to entrust to his beloved Bride, the Church, a memorial of his death and resurrection [Easter Sunday]. (Constitution on the Liturgy, #42)

**Jesus, Church, Eucharist: Sacrament of the Invisible God**
The changes of the past twenty years have led me to broaden somewhat my understanding of what a sacrament is. Besides the traditional seven sacraments which I learned as a child, I now hear people speak of Jesus and the Church as sacraments. I believe what they are saying is this: The invisible God, whose wonder and love are beyond even our imagination, wished to become visible and close to us. God wanted to let us in on God's secret plans for creation. The God who lives in unapproachable light, the source of life and goodness (Eucharistic Prayer IV), spoke the word of creation and the word took flesh and dwelt among us in Jesus of Nazareth. "In him we see our God made visible and so are caught up in love of the God we can not see" (Preface for the Mass of Christmas).

In times past, God revealed this plan, this mysterious sacrament, in bits and pieces through the prophets. But in the fullness of time, in these last days, God has revealed the mystery fully in Jesus (see Hebrews 1:1–2). In Jesus we see God's desire that all things be reconciled and come together in unity. Jesus is God's love made visible, so much so that seeing Jesus is seeing the Father (John 14:9).

While everything that Jesus said and did can be seen as a sacrament of God's mysterious plan, the sacrament we call the Eucharist focuses especially on the paschal mystery of Jesus' passion, death, and resurrection. At Mass, however, when we hear the Holy Thursday words "do this in memory of me," we are told to do not only what Jesus did at the Last Supper but also what Jesus did throughout his entire life: to heal, to teach, to comfort, to be ambassadors of reconciliation (see 2 Corinthians 5:16–21).

We, the Body of Christ, are certainly expected to be part of this sacrament. And this stretches my idea of sacrament. I had always been taught that sacraments are visible signs and instruments of God's invisible grace—channels of God's saving love to the world. I now see that, along with Jesus, we who form the Church are instruments of grace; we are the ordinary way God graces today's world. As Jesus is the sacrament of the invisible God, we who are baptized into Christ become the sacrament which is Church. Indeed, Vatican II speaks of Jesus' "body, the Church, as the universal sacrament of salvation" (Dogmatic Constitution on the Church, #48).

It is at the liturgy and particularly at the Eucharist when the full reality of Christ becomes visible. This means that not only does the Body and Blood of Christ become present under the appearances of bread and wine. But the Body of Christ, the Church, also becomes visible for all to see. The liturgy "is the outstanding means whereby the faithful may express in their lives and manifest to others the mystery of Christ and the real nature of the true Church" (Constitution on the Liturgy, #2). The Eucharist is not only one of the seven sacraments, it is in a sense *the* sacrament—for it contains all that we are, all that the Church is, all that Jesus is and says of God.

### Good Friday: The Holy Sacrifice of the Mass

In our recent Catholic past, Good Friday dominated our understanding of the Eucharist. It was the main image that shaped my eucharistic devotion when I was a child. When I entered the parish church where I grew up, the first thing I saw was a larger-than-life crucifix hanging over the altar.

The Mass is the unbloody sacrifice of Calvary. Being at Mass was like kneeling at the foot of the cross on Calvary. When I was a child my silent reverence at Mass reflected the reverence of Mary and John at the foot of the cross. *Priesthood, altar, sacrifice, offering*—each of these words is part of the vocabulary of the Good Friday dimension of the Mass.

I learned about the Mass and the sacraments from a little book called the *Baltimore Catechism,* which most Catholics my age remember. I remember Question 357: "What is the Mass?" I memorized the answer: "The Mass is the sacrifice of the New Law in which Christ, through the ministry of the priest, offers Himself to God in an unbloody manner under the appearances of bread and wine." Even though I did not understand the full meaning of some of these words, the mention of "sacrifice," "priest," "offering," "blood" brought to my mind the image of Good Friday and permanently associated the Mass with Jesus dying on the cross.

My devotion to the Sacrament was shaped by the image of kneeling at the foot of the cross, gazing at the sacrifice of Jesus, and expressing gratitude for so great a love and sorrow for sins which caused so great a suffering. The image of Good Friday remains an essential element of my understanding of the Eucharist; but while it is essential, it is not enough.

## Holy Thursday: Eucharist as Sacred Banquet

I never thought much about the "meal" aspect of the Mass (the Holy Thursday image) when I was a child. If "Good Friday" was the dominant image in my understanding of the Sacrament of the Eucharist, the image of Holy Thursday and the Lord's Supper was never absent. I knew the Holy Thursday story and many a morning as an altar server I remember kneeling for hours (it seemed like hours) and staring at the picture of the Last Supper carved on the front of the altar at St. Anthony's in Wichita.

I remember that very few people received Holy Communion at weekday Masses, and on Sundays in my parish Holy Communion seemed to be reserved for special groups who went to Communion once a month (the Holy Name Society on one Sunday and the Altar Society on another). But because Good Friday was the dominant (and nearly exclusive) image out of which I understood the Mass, the number of people going to Communion was not an issue. In fact, in those days, very few of us went to communion at all. For many, the Host was to be seen and adored, not eaten.

When I was in grade school, I was one of those "strange" children who went to Holy Communion each morning (and ate breakfast from a little paper bag during first period). But it was only during the 1950s and 1960s when more and more people began to receive holy Communion during Mass that the image of Holy Thursday gradually began to play a larger role in my understanding of the Eucharist.

At that time, too, the "food" of the Eucharist was meager. The Host was small—I never thought of it as bread. And no one drank from the cup. During the 1970s the parish with which I celebrated began to use a Host for the Eucharist that looked and tasted more like real bread. People began to receive Communion in their hands and to drink from the cup. Mass began to look more like a meal. Altars began to look like tables. The prayers of the Mass and the songs we sang spoke openly about eating and drinking, about meals, suppers, and banquets.

All of these things caused the image of Holy Thursday to be added to the image of Good Friday in helping me to understand the Mass. My devotion began to take on a more joyful tone. We began to speak of "celebrating" the Eucharist. To the image of "kneeling at the foot of the cross" I added the image of "sitting with Jesus and the disciples at the Last Supper, listening to his words, sharing the bread and cup."

Not all Catholics experienced this same journey and some hold on to an understanding in which Good Friday is the dominant image. I still think of a woman who asked me after an explanation of the "new Mass": "Father, why are we singing all those happy songs while Jesus is dying on the cross?"

### Easter Sunday: Union with the Risen Lord

If the addition of the Holy Thursday image to Good Friday enriched my understanding of the Eucharist, the addition of the Easter Sunday image has helped me even more. St. Paul, who is perhaps the first Christian to try to explain what the Mass means, was convinced that we, who are baptized into Christ, are the Body of Christ. Not only does the Body and Blood of Christ become present under the appearances of bread and wine, but the Body of Christ, the Church, also becomes visible for all to see.

When St. Paul experienced the Risen Lord at his conversion, he experienced a Christ who was so identified with us that to persecute the Christians was to persecute Christ.

Not just once, but three times the experience is described in the Acts of the Apostles. In chapter nine we see Saul (not yet "St. Paul") terrorizing the followers of Jesus when suddenly, one day on the road to Damascus, Saul "fell to the ground and heard a voice saying to him, 'Saul, Saul, why are you persecuting me?' He said, 'Who are you, sir?' The reply came, 'I am Jesus, whom you are persecuting'" (Acts 9:4–5).

Later Paul himself retells the incident: "I fell to the ground and heard a voice saying to me, 'Saul, Saul, why are you persecuting me?' I replied, 'Who are you, Lord?' Then he said to me, 'I am Jesus of Nazareth whom you are persecuting'" (Acts 22:7–8). Paul tells the story again in chapter twenty-six: "I am Jesus whom you are persecuting" (26:15). The experience revealed to Paul that Christ cannot be separated from his members. The Risen Lord is so united to the Christian that what we do to one another, we do to Christ.

This was the very point that was at issue in Paul's First Letter to the Corinthians, chapter eleven, the earliest written account we have of the Last Supper. When Paul writes to the Corinthians in about the year AD 50, he has some concerns about their "eucharistic devotion":

Now in the following instructions I do not commend you, because when you come together it is not for the better but for the worse. For, to begin with, when you come together as a church, I hear that there are divisions among you; and to some extent I believe it.... What! Do you not have homes to eat and drink in? Or do you show contempt for the church of God and humiliate those who have nothing? What should I say to you? Should I commend you? In this matter I do not commend you! (1 Corinthians 11:17, 22)

Paul reproaches the Corinthians for celebrating the Mass without recognizing the Body of Christ—the poor who go hungry while the rich get drunk. His criticism of their eucharistic devotion is not directed toward some liturgical rule, toward the songs they were singing, or the vestments they were wearing or not wearing, or whether they received Communion standing up or kneeling down—or any of the issues that might disturb some Catholics today—the issue was much more important. They were trying to remember Christ without remembering his Body, which includes the poor and the "unacceptable." They wanted to celebrate the "head" without the "body"—a risen and glorified "sacramental" Christ separated from his actual Body now. Those who worship the glorified Christ in heaven without similar reverence for the members of his Body here on earth "eat and drink judgment" on themselves, as Paul tells the Corinthians. Paul's experience at his conversion had convinced him that the Risen Lord is so identified with the disciples that the two cannot be separated. The Risen Lord is so united to the Christian that what we do to one another, we do to Christ.

St. Paul tells the Corinthians that they must examine themselves as to which body they are celebrating. The Christ they are proclaiming is the Risen Christ, glorified in embers, inseparably united with the poor and suffering. This is the Body they must see in the Eucharist if they are to celebrate worthily, for all who eat and drink without discerning this Body, eat and drink judgment on themselves (see 1 Corinthians 11:29).

This Easter Sunday dimension of the Mass is not a new teaching. St. Augustine reminded his fourth-century parish that: "If then you are the body of Christ and his members, it is your sacrament that reposes on the altar of the Lord…. Be what you see, receive what you are." "There you are on the table, and there you are in the chalice." Paul reminds us of this profound truth. Coming forward at Mass to receive holy Communion is a promise that we will treat each person who receives the bread and drinks the cup as a member of our own body! It is no longer "us and them" but "us." Sharing the meal is a promise that we will treat all men and women as Christ would treat them, indeed as we would treat Christ himself.

This is an enormous responsibility—one which I do not think about enough—and yet one which has greatly influenced the changes in my eucharistic devotion. It is easy to lose sight of this relation: Risen Christ—Mystical Body—Eucharistic Presence. The Mass is not merely a celebration of Real Presence, but a celebration of Real Presence which brings about unity and reconciliation in the whole Body. As the early Christians sang at Mass: As many grapes are brought together and crushed to make the wine—as many grains of wheat are ground into flour to make the one bread—so we, although many, become one Body when we eat the one Bread.

## How Has the Mass Changed?

Even though we celebrate the same Mass today as the apostles, the earliest Christians, the Catholics of the High Middle Ages, and our sainted grandmothers, some things seem different. Some Catholics feel that the Church has changed radically since Vatican II, while others feel that still more change is needed. No matter where you fall along the spectrum, it can be helpful to hear other voices and to grow in your understanding of what has changed, and what remains the same. Once again, Tom Richstatter offers his perspective in the following pages.

***

What happened to Benediction, kneeling for Communion, and silence in church? I have been serving and receiving holy Communion for nearly fifty years. As I look back over that half-century I see that many of the devotions and signs of reverence for the Eucharist that were so dear to me in my younger days I no longer practice! What has happened to my devotion to the most holy Sacrament of the Eucharist?

I have spoken about the Eucharist to many parish groups across the country. And as I listen to the questions and comments of people at these talks, I pick up their concern regarding the changes in eucharistic devotion. Many have experienced changes in their own devotion or witnessed it in others, and they sometimes worry that something important has been lost.

I hope that describing the change in my eucharistic devotion will help many other Catholics to understand and appreciate their own eucharistic devotion and to see the reasons for some of the changes in the devotional practices of their parishes. I'll admit here at the beginning that I am more than a just little scared to talk about my eucharistic devotion. I have been a priest for over twenty-five years and this is certainly not the first time I have talked or written about the Eucharist. Yet it is always difficult to talk openly about something so intimate and so important to me personally—and to you personally.

My devotion to the Eucharist is not something merely external, something that I do; it is something that I am. It lies at the very heart of my identity: how I see myself as a Christian, as a Catholic priest, as an American.

Changes in devotion to the Eucharist affect me—as they affect you—much more deeply than many other changes in my life. To say, "I no longer kneel down when I receive Holy Communion," touches me in a deeper place than to say, "I no longer put salt on my mashed potatoes," although both of these changes in my external behavior are the result of changes in understanding and inner conviction. To explain the changes in external behavior I must talk about the inner changes in belief and understanding.

## What Has Happened to My Eucharistic Devotion?

One way of answering this question is to say that formerly my devotion stopped short; it went only "halfway." My devotion was focused on the first transformation: the transformation of the bread and wine into the Body and Blood of Christ. I had forgotten the warning of St. Paul and did not recognize the second transformation: the transformation of the Christians into Christ. This second transformation is the purpose of the first: Christ becomes really present in the Eucharist so that we may really become his Body. This is precisely what Eucharistic Prayer III is saying when it pleads, "[G]rant that we, who are nourished by the Body and Blood of your Son and filled with his Holy Spirit, may become one body, one spirit in Christ."

I think the second transformation is especially hard for American Catholics. Our American culture places a high value on the individual, on independence and freedom from obligations to one another. I hear people saying, "I have to own a gun because no one is going to protect me but me. The police can't even protect themselves." "I work hard for my money. I am not going to let the government take my money and waste it on welfare. If a culture is infected with racism or sexism, the Christians who are formed by that culture will find it difficult to express devotion to a Eucharist which proclaims that there is "no longer Jew nor Greek, there is no longer slave or free, there is no longer male and female; for all of you are one in Christ Jesus" (Galatians 3:28).

In baptism I renounced "Satan," I renounced racism and sexism and exaggerated individualism and I was born into Christ Jesus. Each time I approach the Eucharist I renew that baptismal promise. As I come to the church for Eucharist, I dip my hand in the baptismal water and renew those baptismal vows. Each time I get up and go to Holy Communion I give a sign to the community that I am committed to all that the Eucharist stands for—I am committed to "do this" in memory of Jesus—to live as he lived, to live no longer for myself but for his Body.

I can't stop halfway: I can't celebrate the transubstantiation of the bread and wine without celebrating Christ's presence in my brothers and sisters. Some Christians still separate the two. I am reminded of the man who once asked me: "Father, why do I have to shake hands with all those people before Holy Communion? I don't know those people; and the ones I know, I don't even like."

## Where Did the Beauty Go?

I remember with nostalgia the magnificence of Solemn High Mass during Forty Hours devotion. I remember the weariness in my little altar boy arms trying to light the dozens of candles on the altars, the smell of the incense, the glitter of the spotlights on the gold threads in the priests' vestments. I remember the monstrance with its jewels which I imagined to be diamonds and rubies and emeralds. The memory is vivid; as a child this was the most glorious thing I had ever seen: the most beautiful room; the most elegant movement; the richest attire. Where did it all go?

If Forty Hours and Solemn Benediction were the high points of the liturgical year then, what is the high point now? The Easter Vigil perhaps? There we experience nervous catechumens sitting around a fire, hearing the stories of creation and salvation—water splashing, wet feet slipping on tile floors, clothes being changed rapidly with the whir of hair dryers in the background, the smell of the oil of Confirmation, breaking bread and sharing a cup for the first time with these new members of the parish. Where did the beauty go? Where is the grandeur? What has happened to my devotion?

I can only say that I am getting a new perspective. I see a new beauty and a new grandeur. It takes a different eye to see my God in the faces of my sisters and brothers with whom I share the broken bread. But there is true beauty there, and I find that beauty can still move me to tears of joy and devotion. Today I judge whether a liturgy is "good" or "bad" not by the number of candles that are lit, nor by the cost of the vestments, nor by whether or not I like the singing.

Today a "good" liturgy is one which transforms me and my fellow parishioners in such a way that men and women of today's society will see the full implication of the sacrament of the Eucharist. And they will say of us as they said of the first Christians, "See how they love one another! There is no one poor among them!"

## *Questions for Reflection*

1. How has your understanding of the Mass changed since your First Communion?

2. Which of these dimensions of the Mass (Good Friday, Holy Thursday, Easter Sunday) most resembles your experience of the Mass?

3. Are there elements of Eucharistic devotion that you miss?

# CHAPTER TWO

# Why Do We Go to Mass?

Now that we have some idea of how to understand what the Mass is, we naturally ask next, "Why do we go?" Why is attendance at Mass such a critical component of our Catholic faith? Is it still the same Mass, even after all the changes of Vatican II, and all the new changes in the Roman Missal? What can this one hour do for our faith and our lives? Once again, Tom Richstatter, O.F.M., uses his own experience to help us consider these questions.

\*\*\*

How many of the things you did when you were ten years old do you still do today? A lot of things I used to do I don't do anymore. This is especially true of physical activities—football is a thing of the past for me.

Even my prayer life has changed. There are some prayers and devotions that I no longer pray. However, Mass remains constant-in my life and in the life of the Church. After two thousand years, God's invitation to the banquet still stands.

In this chapter we'll look at five reasons why we go to Mass.

## *Five Reasons to Go to Mass*

### 1. I need others to pray well.

It is hard to do difficult things alone. And following Jesus can be tough work. One of the reasons why Alcoholics Anonymous, Weight Watchers and other similar programs work is because they are group efforts. To change our lives—in biblical terms, to repent, to convert—we need the help and support of others. At Mass I join with others who are also trying to live the gospel and follow Jesus.

Sometimes when I try to make good decisions—decisions based on gospel values—I get overwhelmed by the extent of social evils in the world. How can I live justly in the midst of so much injustice? How can I live gospel poverty in the midst of so much conspicuous consumption? How can I forgive in a world that seeks vengeance?

At Mass I am reminded and assured that I am not alone in my efforts. I am a member of the Church. I am a member of the Body of Christ. I share in the Spirit of Christ and I am empowered by that Holy Spirit. At each Eucharist I hear the words: "Take this, all of you, and drink from it: for this is the chalice of my Blood, the Blood of the new and eternal covenant, which will be poured out for you and for many for the forgiveness of sins." Together we can make a difference in this world. Together with Christ we can make a tremendous difference. And at Mass we are truly gathered with Christ: "For where two or three are gathered in my name, I am there among them." (Matthew 18:20).

### 2. The Mass enables me to pray with my whole body.

When I pray by myself, at home, I pray mainly with words. I "talk to God"—that's what I was taught prayer is, talking to God. But when I go to Mass, I pray with more than words; I pray with my whole body. I pray with bread and wine, water and oil, coming together and going apart, standing still and processing forward, lighting candles and smelling flowers, even dust and ashes!

At Mass I acknowledge that I am more than just my head or my soul. I am saved body, mind and spirit. And I am saved by a God who is more than just spirit. I am saved by a God who "became flesh and lived among us" (John 1:14). Because of the Incarnation, I can approach God not only with words, but with the elements of my daily life: eating and drinking, sharing meals, and singing songs.

Jesus knows about our daily life because he lived here among us. And he knows about us not just in his head, but in his body. Jesus knew the strain of lifting a heavy table, the sweat of working m the desert sun, the pain of hunger, the embrace of friends, the joyful taste of rich red wine! Consequently, I can pray with earthly things, I pray with symbols.

### Symbol is the language of the Mass.

Symbols don't always come easily for us. Our bishops remind us that American culture "which is oriented to efficiency and production has made us insensitive to the symbolic function of persons and things" (Environment and Art in Catholic Worship, 16). If symbol is the language of the Mass, people who are schooled in the scientific, the practical, and the countable may find it a foreign language, and may find the symbolic nature of the Mass as difficult as speaking a foreign language. They may think that symbols are not real, yet symbols are very real. A kiss between lovers is real communication. It says more than words.

Symbolic language is essential to my prayer life because there are times when mere words are just not enough. Symbols can mean more than a declarative statement or scientific formula or theological dogma.

For example, what does the Mass mean? When I received Holy Communion for the first time at the age of six, I did so with great reverence. I knew what I was doing. I knew what the Mass meant. Today, I certainly know more about the Eucharist than I did then. But the experience of sharing this sacred meal remains the same experience.

It is an experience that is beyond words. I knew what it meant when I was six; I know what it means now; yet the Mass is beyond all those meanings. That is the beauty of the Mass: It means more than we can ever understand it to mean. A symbol says more than mere words could ever say. The Mass is more than words. At Mass I pray with my whole body.

### 3. Besides talking to God, I need God to talk to me.

I often think of prayer as "talking to God," but I have learned from other situations that when I talk too much, I don't learn anything. A real conversation needs not only talking, but also listening. I go to Mass to listen to God speaking to me. I hear Christ's voice in the readings since "it is he himself who speaks when the holy Scriptures are read in the Church" (Constitution on the Sacred Liturgy, 7). I hear Christ's voice in the homily. I hear his voice in the other members of the worshiping assembly—in their devotion, their petitions, their sacrifices. And most especially I hear his voice in the prayers of the Mass.

The Mass is the prayer of the Body of Christ, head and members. The priest always prays in the first-person plural—"we, us"—because it is our prayer, all of us together. We pray "through Christ our Lord" because it is the prayer of Christ united with his Body, the Church. I hear the voice of Christ in the prayers of the Mass.

At each Mass I hear Christ's words "This is my body...this is my blood...do this in memory of me." God speaks to me in these words. I hear proclaimed the reality of the central mystery of faith. I believe that Christ died for our sins, rose from the dead and gives us his body and blood to eat and drink. "For my flesh is true food, and my blood is true drink. Those who eat my flesh and drink my blood abide in me, and I in them" (John 6:55–56).

But the bread does not become just any flesh—it becomes the flesh of Christ the Christ who gave himself up totally for us. It becomes the flesh of Christ who gave his life for the poor, the flesh of Christ who gave up his very life to reveal how much God loves us.

When I hear the words, "Do this in memory of me," I hear God's voice not just challenging me to go to Mass but also challenging me to that self-giving love that the Mass celebrates. We are to become the Body of Christ. We are to live as Christ lived and act as Christ would act. This is the hard part of the Eucharist. The difficult thing is not only believing that the bread and wine become Christ's body and blood; the difficult thing is accepting the challenge to "do this"—to live with that same self-giving love.

After two thousand years, God's invitation to the banquet still stands. We still hear the words "do this...." Yet that challenge is continually modified by the culture and the historical situation into which it is proclaimed. Think about our challenge in Christ's words, "Do this in memory of me."

Here in America, at the beginning of this new millennium, what would Christ do in the face of racism, xenophobia, violence in families, the increasing difference between rich and poor, the inequitable distribution of nature's goods, the struggle of the Church to be holy?

At Mass, when we get up and leave our pew at Communion time and come forward to receive the Bread and drink from the cup, our "Amen" to the words "Body of Christ, Blood of Christ" implies that we accept Christ's challenge.

### 4. Being born again once didn't quite do it.

I know that baptism is a new birth and that in baptism all of my sins are taken away. But I continue to need to hear the words, "Your sins are forgiven." When I go to Mass, I am continually assured of God's ongoing love. Consider how many times during Mass we seek God's mercy! "May almighty God...forgive us our sins" (Penitential Rite); "You take away the sins of the world, have mercy on us" (Glory to God); "To us, also, your servants, who, though sinners, hope in your abundant mercies, graciously grant some share and fellowship with your holy Apostles and Martyrs…and all your Saints: admit us, we beseech you, into their company, not weighing our merits, but granting us your pardon, through Christ our Lord" (Eucharistic Prayer I); "Our Father…forgive us our trespasses as we forgive those who trespass against us" (Lord's Prayer); "Behold the Lamb of God, behold him who takes away away the sins of the world….Lord, I am not worthy…but only say the word and I shall be healed" (Invitation to Communion).

At the heart of each and every Mass we hear Christ's command to "Take this all of you, and drink from it: for this is the chalice of my Blood, the Blood of the new and eternal covenant, which will be poured out for you and for many for the forgiveness of sins."

While I was born again in baptism, I feel a need to be born again, and again, and again. This is why I go to Mass. I promise again, as my parents and godparents promised for me at my baptism, to die to sin, to reject Satan, and all his works and all his empty promises. At each Mass I promise again to follow more closely in the footsteps of Jesus.

Each time I enter the church for Mass I sign myself with water from the baptismal font, or holy water font, to remind myself of my baptism. Mass is the way I renew the promises of my baptism.

Mass is, as one of my friends put it, "the repeatable part of baptism."

When I go to Mass I am assured again of this truth: "Therefore we have been buried with [Christ] by baptism into death, so that, just as Christ was raised from the dead by the glory of the Father, so we too might walk in newness of life" (Romans 6:4). New life: That's what I want from Mass.

### 5. The Mass helps me find the sacred in the ordinary.

Do you receive those Christmas form letters where your friends tell you all the exciting things they have done in the past year? I get lots of those letters. I send them out myself!

But while, in a good year, there may be a couple exciting events, most of my life is ordinary. We can talk about "new life" and "life in the Risen Lord," but most of my life is simply routine. I get up, go to work, come home, go to bed.

If Christianity is going to have any real influence on my life it must touch me in the ordinary and the routine. At Mass we use ordinary things: eating and drinking, standing and sitting, shaking hands and keeping quiet. In this ordinary stuff, I find God.

Once, when parishioners asked St. Augustine (AD 354–430) what had happened to all the miracles they read about in the Gospels—feeding thousands with a few loaves and raising the dead to life—St. Augustine asked them to think of the grain of wheat falling to the ground and producing stalk and blade.

Where can you find a greater miracle than that! Often the greatest miracles are to be found in the ordinary.

The Mass is the principal element in my life that has helped me develop a "spirit of wonder and awe" in the presence of the ordinary. Remember the words that St. Augustine offered his parishioners: "If then you are the body of Christ and his members, it is your sacrament that reposed on the altar of the Lord.... Be what you see and receive what you are" (Sermon 272). "There you are on the table, and there you are in the chalice" (Sermon 229).

At the Mass my ordinary life is taken up into God's great plan for the world. The Second Vatican Council says that Mass "is the outstanding means whereby the faithful may express in their lives and manifest to others the mystery of Christ and the real nature of the true Church" (Constitution on the Sacred Liturgy, 2). At Mass we not only hear of God's dreams for us, we act them out: We are taken up into those dreams.

I hear of God's dreams of justice for all peoples of all nations. In Holy Communion I see how the Body and Blood of the Lord are broken and shared and how everyone receives enough—the rich and the poor, young and old, hungry and weak. I am forced by the contrast between the Table of the Lord and the table of this world (where very few have enough-indeed millions are starving!) to rethink my ideas of justice and charity. At Mass, we don't just pray, "Thy kingdom come," we experience what the kingdom promises. We don't just talk about Holy Thursday, we eat and drink. We not only talk about Good Friday, we are sacrifice. We not only attend Easter liturgies, we are risen in the promise of Christ. At Mass, our lives are taken up into the paschal victory of Christ.

At Mass our ordinary daily lives are taken up into eternity. What we do at Mass is but a hint of what we will be doing forever in heaven when, "freed at last from the wound of corruption and made fully into a new creation, we shall sing to you with gladness" (Eucharistic Prayer, Reconciliation I).

In the new world where fullness of God's peace will be revealed we will be seated at table with "our brothers and sisters and those of every race and tongue...to share with them the unending banquet of unity in a new heaven and a new earth where the fullness of your peace will shine forth" (Eucharistic Prayer, Reconciliation II). That's why I go to Mass!

## Questions for Reflection

1. Why do you go to Mass?
2. What part of the Mass speaks to you most strongly? Why?
3. How do you bring the Eucharist into your daily life?

# CHAPTER THREE

# How Do We Go to Mass?

Now that we understand what the Mass is and what it can do for us, we might still have some questions about just what to do when we get there. Whether you've been away from the table for a while or are a daily communicant, the new translation of the Roman Missal means that there will be some changes for all of us. Just how significant are these changes? Will lifelong Catholics still recognize the Mass? Why are these changes necessary?

Fr. Lawrence Mick has written about the changes in the Roman Missal and what it means for our experience of the Mass.

\*\*\*

## *Changing How We Pray*

There has been much written in recent years about the revision in the language we use at the liturgy. Some of the concern that has been expressed arises fro the perception that these changes are part of a larger trend in the Church to reverse the renewal of the liturgy that was mandated by the Second Vatican Council in its Constitution on the Sacred Liturgy. Some writers have rejoiced in this prospect, while others have been deeply depressed by it.

But, even a quick look at the new changes reveals that they are not a major reversal of the post–Vatican II reforms. This is a new translation of the Mass, not a new ritual for celebrating the Eucharist. The Mass will still have the same parts, the same patterns and the same flow as it has had for the past several decades. It is only the translation of the Latin that has changed. But it has changed in some significant parts of the liturgy, so congregations will notice that something is new.

### Entrance Rites

One of the most publicized of the new texts occurs just after the Mass begins and recurs several times throughout the Mass. Whenever the priest says, "The Lord be with you," the new assembly response will be, "And with your spirit." This is a more direct translation of the Latin and matches what many other language groups have been using for years. It will obviously take some adjustment, since we are used to saying, "And also with you," but it is a minor change.

There are also some changes to the penitential rite. The *Confiteor* (I Confess) has been revised, again to match the Latin more closely. Those who are old enough to remember reading along in their Sunday missals when the Mass was celebrated in Latin may recognize the new wording, which puts more stress on our unworthiness than the current text. It now says, "I have greatly sinned" and later adds, "through my fault, through my fault, through my most grievous fault."

The other two options for the Penitential Rite have also been revised. The second form, which has gotten little use till recent years, will now read as follows: The priest says, "Have mercy on us, O Lord." The people respond, "For we have sinned against you." Then the priest says, "Show us, O Lord, your mercy," and the people respond, "And grant us your salvation."

The third form of this rite, with the various invocations of Christ (e.g., "You came to call sinners") will be much the same, though an option is added to conclude each invocation in Greek: *"Kyrie eleison, Christe eleison Kyrie eleison,"* rather than the English: "Lord, have mercy; Christ, have mercy; Lord, have mercy." The first two forms conclude with this threefold litany, too, either in English or in Greek.

The Glory to God (Gloria) has been significantly changed, with more words and many lines rearranged. Some of those lines had been abbreviated in the most recent version because they were rather repetitive, but such repetition is not inappropriate in a hymn of praise to God. Since this is a hymn, composers will have to create new musical settings of the Glory to God for us to learn.

## The Gloria

Glory to God in the highest,
and on earth peace to people of good will.

We praise you,
we bless you,
we adore you,
we glorify you,
we give you thanks for your great glory,
Lord God, heavenly King,
O God, almighty Father.

Lord Jesus Christ, Only Begotten Son,
Lord God, Lamb of God, Son of the Father,
you take away the sins of the world,

have mercy on us;
you take away the sins of the world,

receive our prayer;

you are seated at the right hand of the father,

   have mercy on us.

For you alone are the Holy One.

you alone are the Lord,

you alone are the Most High,

Jesus Christ,

with the Holy Spirit,

in the Glory of God the Father.

Amen.

### Liturgy of the Word

There are only two texts that change in the people's parts in the Liturgy of the Word. One is very small; the other is quite large. The small one is the response before the Gospel, where we will respond again, "And with your spirit," when the priest or deacon says, "The Lord be with you."

The bigger changes come in the text of the Creed (Profession of Faith). The first obvious change is with the first word. We used to begin with, "We believe," while the revised text has, "I believe." When the last translation was prepared, the scholars decided to use the plural because the original text of the Creed (in both Latin and Greek) proclaimed by the Councils of Nicaea and Constantinople in the fourth century used the plural. But the Latin text in the missal is in the singular, perhaps because it came into the Mass from the Baptismal Rite, where the one being baptized made an individual profession of faith. The use of the singular could remind us of our baptism, though here we are clearly professing our faith as an assembly rather than as individuals.

Another noticeable change comes in the line about the Son's divinity. We used to say he is "one in being with the Father." The new text says he is "consubstantial with the Father." *Consubstantial* is not really a translation. It is a transliteration—the same Latin word, spelled in English—of the Latin *consubstantialis,* which means "one in being." Whether translation or transliteration, the point is that Jesus is God, one with the Father.

Another change appears when we speak of Christ's human nature. We used to say, "by the power of the Holy Spirit he was born of the Virgin Mary and became man." The new text says, "and by the Holy Spirit was incarnate of the Virgin Mary and became man." *Incarnate* means "enfleshed," so using the term here reminds us that he was human from the moment of his conception, not just at his birth.

There are several other minor changes in the text of the Creed. It will no doubt take us a while to commit the new version to memory so that we can profess it together easily. The new missal also allows the option of using the Apostles' Creed instead of the Nicene Creed, especially during Lent and Easter. The Apostles' Creed is another ancient Christian creed, long in use by Roman

Catholics in our baptismal promises. Those who pray the rosary will also recognize it.

## Liturgy of the Eucharist

During the Preparation of the Gifts, the prayers of the priest have several changes, but the only change for the assembly is the addition of the word holy to the response just before the Prayer over the Offerings. Where we used to say, "for our good and the good of all his Church," the new text says, "for our good and the good of all his holy Church."

When the Eucharistic Prayer begins, we will again respond, "And with your spirit," to the first line of the opening dialogue. The last line of that dialogue also changes. We used to say, "It is right to give him thanks and praise," but the new text is simply, "It is right and just." This will lead more clearly into the opening of the prefaces, which will commonly begin with the words, "It is truly right and just."

There is only one change in the Holy, Holy. Where we used to say, "God of power and might," the new text has "God of hosts." While this may make many people think of round Communion wafers, the meaning here is "armies," and it refers to the armies of angels who serve God.

## The Creed

I believe in one God,
the Father almighty,
maker of heaven and earth,
of all things visible and invisible.

I believe in one Lord Jesus Christ,
the Only Begotten Son of God,
born of the Father before all ages.
God from God, Light from Light,
true God from true God,
begotten, not made, consubstantial with the Father;
through him all things were made.
For us men and for our salvation
he came down from heaven,
*(all bow for the next two lines)*
and by the Holy Spirit was incarnate of the Virgin Mary,
and became man.

For our sake he was crucified under Pontius Pilate,
he suffered death and was buried,
and rose again on the third day
in accordance with the Scriptures.
He ascended into heaven
and is seated at the right hand of the Father.
He will come again in glory

to judge the living and the dead
and his kingdom will have no end.

I believe in the Holy Spirit, the Lord, the giver of life,
who proceeds from the Father and the Son,
who with the Father and the Son is adored and glorified,
who has spoken through the prophets.

I believe in one, holy, catholic and apostolic Church.
I confess one Baptism for the forgiveness of sins
and I look forward to the resurrection of the dead
and the life of the world to come. Amen.

The Memorial Acclamations have all been changed, too. The one
that is most familiar to us (Christ has died, Christ is risen...) has
disappeared completely. The three remaining ones are similar to
those in the previous missal, but the wording is different in each
case.

There is no change to our final "Amen." *Amen* is in fact a
Hebrew word that has been kept in the original for centuries.

In the Communion Rite, there are only two changes in the
assembly's responses. At the Sign of Peace, we find again, "And
with your spirit," instead of "And also with you." When the priest
invites us to share in the Lord's supper, we will respond, "Lord, I
am not worthy that you should enter under my roof, but only say
the word and my soul shall be healed."

The use of "under my roof" is a reference to the Gospel passage where the centurion asks Jesus to heal his servant but says he is not worthy for Jesus to enter his house (Luke 7:6). The other change is "my soul" instead of "I," which focuses more clearly on the spiritual dimension of the healing we seek.

At the dismissal, we find the final "And with your spirit." There are some new forms of the dismissal for the priest to use, but the assembly's final response stays the same: "Thanks be to God."

While these changes have required us to learn some new language, the arrival of the new missal offers us a prime opportunity to deepen our understanding and appreciation of the Mass. That's why you may find a variety of forms of catechesis about the Mass offered in your parish and online as we implement the new texts. Taking advantage of these opportunities is more important than debating the value of the new texts.

In the words of Vatican II's *Lumen Gentium,* #11, the Eucharist is the "source and summit" of Christian life. Anything we can do to understand our liturgy more deeply will draw us closer to God.

## *The Order of Mass*

The changes in the translation of the Roman Missal affect several parts of the Mass. In order to put these changes into context and to offer an introduction to, or a refresher of, the parts of the Mass for new or inactive Catholics, we've outlined the Order of the Mass below. In keeping with our discussion of the Mass as a meal (see chapter one), Carol Leubering offers some helpful ways to think about the various parts of the Mass.

## The Introductory Rites

Beginning with the Entrance Processional, the Introductory Rites are like gathering the whole family together for a holiday meal. Once everyone has arrived, we begin the Mass with the Sign of the Cross and greet one another. This is where we change our, "And also with you," to, "And with your spirit." Next is the Penitential Act (the Confiteor, or I Confess), where we acknowledge our faults and put aside our differences in a spirit of family unity. The Kyrie (Lord, Have Mercy) and the Gloria follow.

## The Liturgy of the Word

We can think of this part of the Mass as telling the family story. It echoes the Jewish tradition of telling the story of Israel's liberation on the night of Passover, but we might more readily relate to our own memories of sharing childhood stories or tales of favorite uncles or strange cousins. We have heard all the stories before (just as we should not be surprised by any of the readings of Scripture we hear at Mass), but somehow we all feel a greater sense of unity when we share them again. After the readings and the Homily, we all share our faith together when we recite the Creed.

## The Liturgy of the Eucharist

Most family gatherings involve a meal. Whether it's last-minute takeout or an elaborate Thanksgiving feast, sharing food and drink together is what makes us feel most at home and comfortable in one another's company. At Mass, the priest guides us through the Eucharistic Prayer and the Communion Rite (including the Sign of Peace) and invites us all to the heavenly banquet.

### The Concluding Rites

Just as when we take our leave from a family meal, the Con-cluding Rites signal that Mass has ended. Of course, there are a few who like to linger for a few more moments of reflection or one more prayer, but this is familiar to those who have a favorite aunt who just hates to say good-bye at the holidays. Our family gatherings celebrate our unity and our love and leave us nourished in body and spirit. Without forgetting about its other important dimensions (see the discussion of Good Friday and Easter Sunday in chapter one), thinking of the Mass as a family meal can help us approach the celebration with a spirit of joy. Even if some of the details have changed, the important thing is that we all remember to gather and share, in our families, and in our faith.

## Questions for Reflection

1. Why do we say the Creed together?
2. Why does Vatican II call the Eucharist the "source and summit" of Christian life?
3. How do you feel about the new words we say at Mass?

# *Conclusion*

The Mass has always been the central celebration of our Catholic faith. Over the millennia, it has been celebrated in many ways. It was celebrated in the catacombs beneath the city of Rome during the persecutions; it has been offered at cathedrals designed and decorated by the likes of Michelangelo; it has been recited alone in prison cells by heroic priests; it is still recited nearly alone in churches all over the country where other heroic priests continue to open the church doors to waning congregations.

If you are new to the Church, your experience of Mass will change and grow as your faith does. If you're a cradle Catholic, you can attest to this truth. But no matter how each individual understands the Mass, no matter how the details of the language change, the Mass we celebrate today is the same, "the Mass of all ages," as the *Catechism of the Catholic Church* proclaims.

Blessed are those called to the supper of the Lamb!

# *Sources*

Some of the information in this book originally appeared in:

*Becoming Catholic: An Adult's Faith Journey.* Catholic Update video.

*Eucharist: Celebrating Christ Present.* Catholic Update video.

*First Communion.* Catholic Update video.

Luebering, Carol. "First Communion: Joining the Family Table." *Catholic Update*, April, 1995.

Mick, Lawrence E. "Changing How We Pray: A Guide to the New Translation of the Roman Missal." *Catholic Update*, August 2010.

Richstatter, Thomas, O.F.M. "The Sacrament of the Eucharist: What Has Happened to My Devotion?" *Catholic Update*, September 1992.

_____. "Why I Go to Mass." *Catholic Update*, August 2002.

Shannon, William H. "Eucharist: Understanding Christ's Body." *Catholic Update*, January 1999.

VonLehmen, Jeffrey D. "Real Presence in the Eucharist." *Catholic Update,* September 1996.

*A Walk Through the Mass.* Catholic Update video.

# Contributors

**Carol Luebering** is an author whose books include *Handing on the Faith: Your Child's First Communion* and *Coping With Loss: Praying Your Way to Acceptance.*

**Thomas Richstatter**, O.F.M., has a doctorate in liturgy and sacramental theology from the Institut Catholique of Paris. A popular writer and lecturer, Fr. Richstatter teaches courses on the sacraments at St. Meinrad (Indiana) School of Theology.

**William H. Shannon** is professor emeritus of history at Nazareth College, Rochester, New York, and founder of the International Thomas Merton Society. His books include *Exploring the Catechism of the Catholic Church, Thomas Merton: An Introduction,* and *Here on the Way to There: A Catholic Perspective on Dying and What Follows.*

**Jeffrey D. VonLehmen** is pastor of St. Pius X Church in Edgewood, Kentucky.

**Lawrence E. Mick** is a priest of the archdiocese of Cincinnati. He holds a master's degree in liturgical studies from the University of Notre Dame. He is the author of over five hundred articles.